1/21

Wilbraham Public Library
Crane Park Drive
Wilbraham, MA 01095

D1561289

ALL AROUND THE WORLD
GREECE

by Kristine Spanier

po go

Ideas for Parents and Teachers

Pogo Books let children practice reading informational text while introducing them to nonfiction features such as headings, labels, sidebars, maps, and diagrams, as well as a table of contents, glossary, and index.

Carefully leveled text with a strong photo match offers early fluent readers the support they need to succeed.

Before Reading

- "Walk" through the book and point out the various nonfiction features. Ask the student what purpose each feature serves.
- Look at the glossary together. Read and discuss the words.

Read the Book

- Have the child read the book independently.
- Invite him or her to list questions that arise from reading.

After Reading

- Discuss the child's questions. Talk about how he or she might find answers to those questions.
- Prompt the child to think more. Ask: Greeks began building columns into structures long ago. Have you noticed columns on important buildings where you live?

Pogo Books are published by Jump!
5357 Penn Avenue South
Minneapolis, MN 55419
www.jumplibrary.com

Copyright © 2020 Jump!
International copyright reserved in all countries.
No part of this book may be reproduced in any form without written permission from the publisher.

Library of Congress Cataloging-in-Publication Data

Names: Spanier, Kristine, author.
Title: Greece / by Kristine Spanier.
Description: Minneapolis, MN: Jump, 2020.
Series: All around the world
Includes bibliographical references and index.
Identifiers: LCCN 2018041733 (print)
LCCN 2018043732 (ebook)
ISBN 9781641286435 (ebook)
ISBN 9781641286411 (hardcover : alk. paper)
ISBN 9781641286428 (pbk.)
Subjects: LCSH: Greece—Juvenile literature.
Classification: LCC DF717 (ebook)
LCC DF717 .S67 2019 (print) | DDC 949.5—dc23
LC record available at https://lccn.loc.gov/2018041733

Editor: Susanne Bushman
Designer: Molly Ballanger

Photo Credits: Offcaania/Shutterstock, cover; Neirfy/Shutterstock, 1; Pixfiction/Shutterstock, 3; alxpin/iStock, 4; Olga_Gavrilova/iStock, 5; Valery Bocman/Shutterstock, 6-7; VogelSP/iStock, 8-9; Antonio Gravante/Shutterstock, 10; saiko3p/Shutterstock, 11; Vasilis Protopapas/iStock, 12-13; DeAgostini/SuperStock, 14-15l; 12_Tribes/Shutterstock, 14-15m; Miroshnichenko Tetiana/Shutterstock, 14-15r; volkova natalia/Shutterstock, 14-15 background; ConstantinosZ/Shutterstock, 16t; Karl Allgaeuer/Shutterstock, 16b; bhofack2/iStock, 17; LOUISA GOULIAMAKI/AFP/Getty Images, 18-19; Laszlo Szirtesi/Shutterstock, 20-21; RomanR/Shutterstock, 23.

Printed in the United States of America at Corporate Graphics in North Mankato, Minnesota.

TABLE OF CONTENTS

CHAPTER 1

WELCOME TO GREECE!

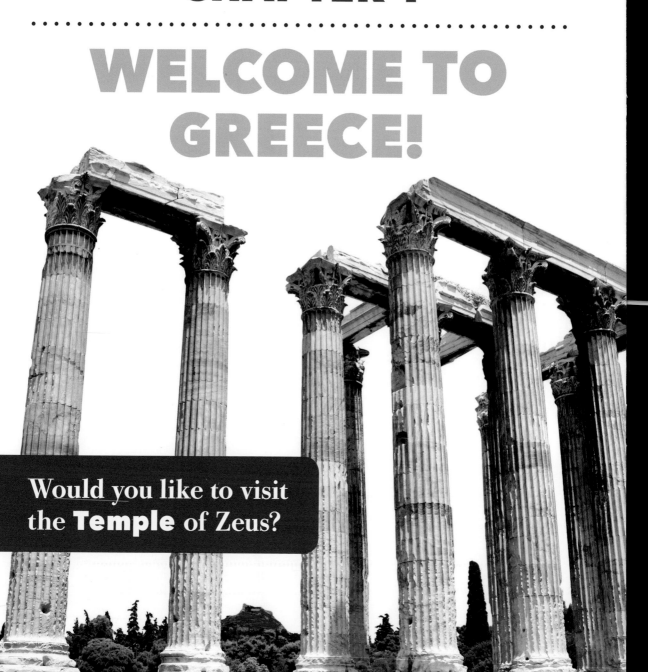

Would you like to visit the **Temple** of Zeus?

Or go to the Cyclades Islands? Then you would enjoy Greece. Let's visit!

Vikos Gorge

Greece has more than 2,000 islands. Crete is the largest. Some islands grow olive trees. Greece grows the most olive types of any country.

The Pindus Mountains run through the mainland. Vikos **Gorge** is there. It is one of the deepest gorges in the world. How deep is it? Almost 3,300 feet (1,006 meters)! Mount Olympus is in the east. It is the highest point. It is 9,570 feet (2,917 m) high.

DID YOU KNOW?

Many people work on boats here. They ship **exports**. They work on cruise ships. Ferries. Fishing boats. Why? Many Greeks live on the coast.

Athens is the **capital**. It is one of the oldest cities in Europe. People have lived here for about 5,000 years!

The people elect a **parliament**. The **prime minister** leads the government.

WHAT DO YOU THINK?

Athens had the first **democracy**. All men could vote. Others couldn't. Like who? Enslaved people. Women. Children. Do you think everyone should be able to vote? Why or why not?

Athens

CHAPTER 2

A LONG HISTORY

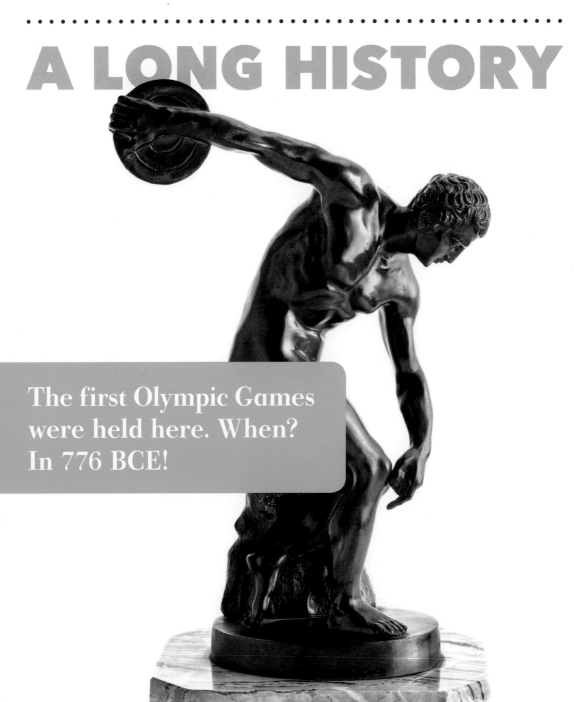

The first Olympic Games were held here. When? In 776 BCE!

Walls surround parts of the city of Rhodes. Why? To protect it from **invaders**. When were they built? More than 700 years ago!

wall

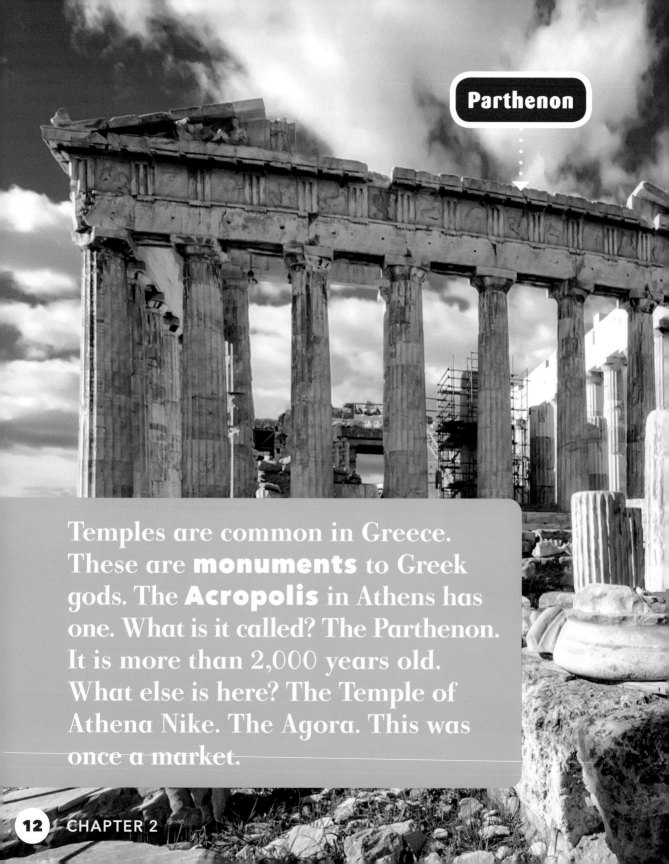

Parthenon

Temples are common in Greece. These are **monuments** to Greek gods. The **Acropolis** in Athens has one. What is it called? The Parthenon. It is more than 2,000 years old. What else is here? The Temple of Athena Nike. The Agora. This was once a market.

TAKE A LOOK!

Classical Greek **architecture** has special features. Like what? Columns. The Greeks were the first to use them. Look at the other parts. Have you seen these on other buildings?

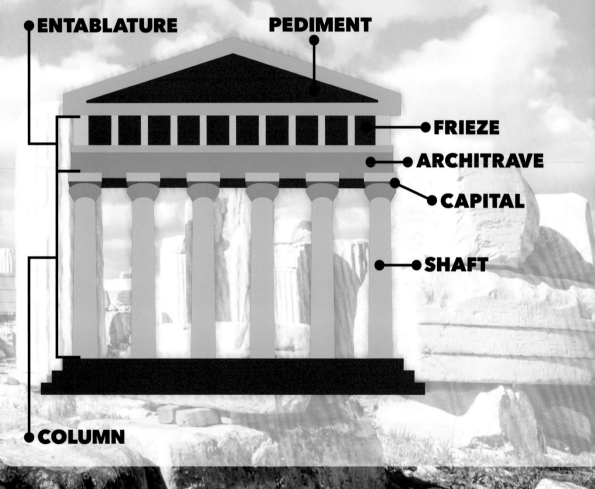

ENTABLATURE

PEDIMENT

FRIEZE

ARCHITRAVE

CAPITAL

SHAFT

COLUMN

Ancient Greeks added to the world's knowledge. In what subjects? Science. **Philosophy**. The arts. Pottery was covered in images. What did they show? Greek **myths**!

CHAPTER 3

LIFE IN GREECE

Do you like olives? Or pita bread? These are popular foods in Greece. Souvlaki is a meat kebab. Try dolmades. These are grape leaves stuffed with rice and spices.

souvlaki

dolmades

Would you like to try a gyro? This is meat, onions, tomatoes, and yogurt sauce. Wrapped in what? Pita bread! Yum!

gyro

Children here start school by the age of six. They must attend until they are at least 15. They take field trips to ancient sites. Museums, too. Students learn English. They also learn French or German. Later, students can choose to move on to high school.

WHAT DO YOU THINK?

Men here do nine months of **military** service. When? At age 19. Some are in college. They do their service after they finish. Do you think military service should be required?

Sports are popular here. Which ones? Soccer and basketball. Athletes run in foot races. They ski in the mountains. They also swim and windsurf.

Greeks make art, too. They make **textiles** and pottery. Or they create silver jewelry.

Greece is a place of wonder. Would you like to visit?

QUICK FACTS & TOOLS

GREECE

Location: southern Europe

Size: 50,949 square miles
(131,957 square kilometers)

Population: 10,761,523
(July 2018 estimate)

Capital: Athens

Type of Government:
parliamentary republic

Language: Greek

Exports: food and beverages,
olives, manufactured goods

Currency: Euro

GLOSSARY

Acropolis: The highest point in a Greek city where important temples and monuments were built.

ancient: Very old.

architecture: A style of building.

capital: A city where government leaders meet.

democracy: A form of government in which the people choose their leaders in elections.

exports: Products sold to different countries.

gorge: A deep valley with steep, rocky sides.

invaders: People who enter an area for conquest or plunder.

military: The armed forces of a country.

monuments: Statues, buildings, or other structures that remind people of events or people.

myths: Old stories that express the beliefs or history of a group of people.

parliament: A group of people elected to make laws.

philosophy: The study of truth, wisdom, knowledge, and the nature of reality.

prime minister: The leader of a country.

temple: A building used for worship.

textiles: Woven or knitted fabrics or cloths.

Greece's currency

INDEX

TO LEARN MORE

Finding more information is as easy as 1, 2, 3.

1 Go to www.factsurfer.com

2 Enter "Greece" into the search box.

3 Click the "Surf" button to see a list of websites.

FACT SURFER